NATURAL WORLD
GOLDEN EAGLE

HABITATS • LIFE CYCLES • FOOD CHAINS • THREATS

Malcolm Penny

RAINTREE
STECK-VAUGHN
PUBLISHERS

A Harcourt Company

Austin   New York
www.raintreesteckvaughn.com

NATURAL WORLD

Chimpanzee • Crocodile • Black Rhino • Dolphin • Elephant
Giant Panda • Giraffe • Golden Eagle • Great White Shark
Grizzly Bear • Hippopotamus • Killer Whale • Leopard • Lion
Orangutan • Penguin • Polar Bear • Tiger

Cover: A male golden eagle in the borders of Scotland.
Title page: A golden eagle in flight.
Contents page: Perching on an old pine branch on moorland.
Index page: A golden eagle looks out over its territory in Siberia.

Published by Raintree Steck-Vaughn Publishers, an imprint of Steck-Vaughn Company

Library of Congress Cataloging-in-Publication Data is available upon request.

Printed in Italy. Bound in the United States.

1 2 3 4 5 6 7 8 9 0 LB 05 04 03 02 01

Picture acknowledgments
Ancient Art & Architecture Collection 37 Ronald Sheridan; *Ardea* 9 N.N. Birks, 10 Uno Berggren, 11, 13 S. Roberts, 14-15 Uno Berggren, 15 R.T. Smith, 18, 19 Eric Dragesco, 22 Francois Gohier, 32 Eric Dregesco, 34 Uno Berggren, 39 P. Morris, 42 Uno Berggren, 44t S. Roberts, 44m Eric Dragesco; *Bruce Coleman* 8 Pacific Stock, 17 Erwin & Peggy Bauer, 35 Pacific Stock, 38 Geoff Dove, 48 Bruce Coleman inc; *Corbis* 28 Perry Conway, 40 Dean Conger; *FLPA* 29 Fritz Polking, 30 Silvestris, 31 Ofer Bahat; *Getty Images* 24, 45t Bruno Dittrich; *NHPA* **Title page** Stephen Dalton, 6 John Shaw, 7 Eric Soder, 16 Laurie Campbell, 20 Stephen Dalton, 23 John Shaw, 26 Eric Soder, 36 Laurie Campbell, 41 Hellio & Van Ingen, 44b John Shaw; *Oxford Scientific Films* **Cover** Niall Benvie, 21 Mike Brown; *Windrush Photos* 33, 45b David Hill; *Woodfall Wild Images* 12, 43, 44m Stuart Rae.
Artwork by Michel Posen.

Contents

Meet the Golden Eagle

The golden eagle is one of the largest and most powerful birds of prey. It was once common over most of the northern hemisphere, but since the 1950s, it has become vulnerable over a large part of its range. Its home is usually in highland or mountainous areas.

In North America, the golden eagle lives from Mexico to Alaska, across to Newfoundland and down to North Carolina. In Europe, it ranges from Scotland, through Norway to Spain, Italy, and the Balkans. Some live in north-west Africa, but they are more commonly found in Russia, and down through Asia as far as southern China and Japan.

GOLDEN EAGLE FACTS

The golden eagle is named after the wash of golden feathers across its head and neck. Its scientific name is *Aquila chrysaetos*, which comes from the Latin word for "eagle," *aquila*, and the Greek word for "golden eagle," *chrysaetos*.

●

Adult females are about 3.3 feet (1 meter) long, with a wingspan of up to 7.5 feet (2.3 meters). They weigh between 8 to 14 pounds (3.8 and 6.6 kilograms). As in most birds of prey, the adult male is slightly smaller and quite a lot lighter, weighing between 6 to 10 pounds (2.8 and 4.5 kilograms).

Feathers
The feathers fan out for landing.

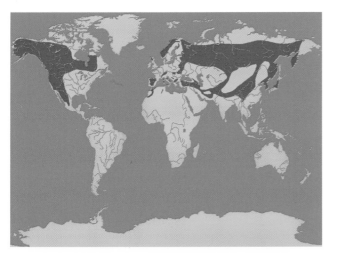

▲ The areas shaded red show where golden eagles live in the wild.

Wings
The wings are broad and strong. They can carry heavy loads of up to 10 pounds (4.5 kilograms).

Bill
The golden eagle's bill is sharp-edged and hooked, for cutting and tearing flesh.

Eyes
Golden eagles have large eyes and excellent eyesight for spotting prey.

Feet
Golden eagles have powerful feet with huge, sharp claws, or talons, for killing and gripping prey.

Legs
The golden eagle's legs are fully feathered, which is why it is in a group called "booted eagles."

► An adult golden eagle

World of the Golden Eagle

Golden eagles live mainly in mountainous areas, where they can find wide, open hunting grounds. Their homes are usually in remote places, far from human settlements. A golden eagle needs cliffs with rocky ledges to use as look-out points, from which it can survey its huge territory. It also uses cliffs for nesting. Where there are no cliffs, it nests in large trees. In Europe, golden eagles are also found hunting in forests and over wetlands.

▼ A mountain goat sits high up in the Central Rocky Mountains in Colorado. Remote mountains and foothills make an ideal habitat for golden eagles.

▲ An Alpine marmot on the look-out for dangerous predators in Switzerland. Golden eagles often eat marmots.

Neighbors

In North America, golden eagles soar over rocky crags where mountain goats live. Woodchucks and ground squirrels hide among the rocks. In Europe, chamois (goat-like animals), marmots and mountain hares share the slopes with the eagles. In both Europe and North America, highland birds such as grouse and ptarmigan feed among the heather. All of these animals may become the eagles' prey.

The Eagle's Relatives

There are different species of eagles all over the world. Most of them are agile and powerful hunters. They are all members of the same group of large birds of prey, which includes hawks and buzzards. The bald eagle once lived all over North America. It became very rare in the 1960s, although its numbers are now recovering.

OTHER NAMES

The golden eagle's closest relatives are known as "booted eagles," because they have feathers all the way down to their feet. However some people prefer to call them "rough-legged eagles," which is probably a better name because there is another bird called the booted eagle.

▲ A wedge-tailed eagle in Australia. The wedge-tailed eagle is respected by farmers because it kills large numbers of rabbits, which are a pest in Australia.

◄ A bald eagle swoops down on some fish it has seen, with its talons outstretched. The bald eagle is mainly a scavenger, but it is also good at catching fish in shallow water.

In Africa, the fish eagle is a similar-looking bird to the golden eagle, with a white head and black body. It catches its prey with a dramatic swoop over the water. The biggest of the eagle's close relatives is the wedge-tailed eagle, with a wingspan of over 8 feet (2.5 meters). It lives in Australia. The smallest eagle, with a wingspan of 5 feet (1.5 meters), is the lesser spotted eagle, which migrates between Europe and southern Africa.

The harpy eagle lives in forests from southern Mexico, through the Amazon region to southern Brazil. It is immensely powerful, feeding mainly on large parrots, but quite able to kill and carry off a three-toed sloth weighing 9 pounds (4 kilograms). The strongest eagle of all is Pallas's sea eagle. This eagle was once seen carrying a fish weighing 13 pounds (6 kilograms). The bird itself weighs less than 7.7 pounds (3.5 kilograms).

An Eagle is Born

It is spring, and a pregnant female eagle turns uncomfortably in her nest, high up on a cliff ledge, ready to lay her eggs. The eggs have been growing inside her for several weeks. Eventually, in late March or early April, she lays the first of her two eggs. Three or four days later, she lays her second egg. If she has three eggs, the third will arrive another three or four days later.

▶ One egg is usually more spotted than the other.

▼ A golden eagle nest will be used for years by the pair that built it. They add new sticks and twigs every year.

At first, both the mother and father eagle take turns to incubate the clutch of eggs. But as the time for hatching comes closer, the female takes over the duty of keeping them warm. About 40–45 days later, the eggs begin to hatch, in the order in which they were laid.

EAGLE EGGS

Eagles usually lay two eggs, sometimes one and rarely three.

•

The eggs range from pure white to a blotchy brown color and measure about 2 inches (6 cm) wide and 3 inches (8 cm) long.

•

A group of eggs is called a clutch.

The hatchling

Like most hatching chicks, the eaglet has a tool to help it break through the thick eggshell and find its way into the open. The egg-tooth, as it is called, is a hard knob on the end of the tiny bird's bill. With it, the chick can force open a crack in the shell, until the gap is big enough for it to crawl out.

◀ This golden eagle chick is only four weeks old.

EAGLE CHICKS

Newly hatched eagles are called hatchlings, nestlings, chicks, or eaglets. They are about 5.9 inches (15 cm) tall and weigh about 1.8 ounces (50 grams).

•

In eight out of ten golden eagle nests, the first chick to hatch is the only one to survive.

The newly hatched eaglets are weak and clumsy, and only lightly covered in pure-white down. Their mother needs to keep them warm for the first two weeks of their life, because they usually live high up in mountainous areas, where the weather is often quite cold, even in spring.

After a few days, a thicker layer of downy feathers gradually replaces the first, thin layer. Three or four weeks later, this layer is replaced by feathers. The first feathers are brown and streaky, unlike their parents' plain brown plumage.

▲ It seems strange that birds who nest in such cold places should have chicks so poorly covered in down.

Nestlings

Their father helps to brood the newly hatched eaglets when they are very tiny, but soon he sets off to hunt for food for them, leaving the brooding to their mother. He does not feed the chicks himself. Instead, he brings the food to their mother, who uses her huge, sharp bill to tear it into small pieces for the eaglets to eat. She is amazingly gentle with her tiny chicks, pulling off tiny strips of meat and offering them to the chicks' open mouths.

The young eaglets are not gentle with each other. They fight fiercely for each morsel of food and the elder, larger one nearly always wins. The elder chick also bullies its younger brothers or sisters, pecking and jostling them, even when they are not being fed. The result is that the younger eaglets often die, because they do not get enough to eat. Only the eldest, the first to hatch, survives. But in years when there is plenty of food, the younger birds will also survive. By having hatching more than one chick, eagles are able to take advantage of years when there are good food supplies.

▶ With a bill that could swallow the chick whole, the female feeds it delicate strips of meat.

▼ A male eagle carries food to female, who is waiting on the nest.

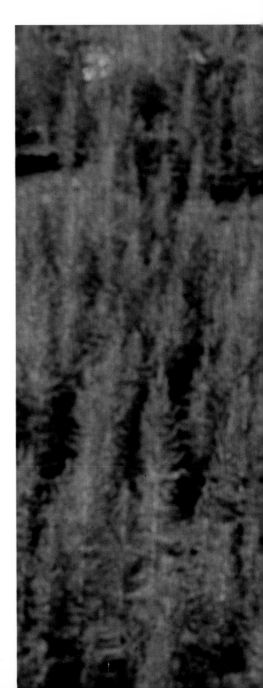

14

MALE EAGLES

Most male birds of prey, including the golden eagle, are smaller and lighter than the females. This makes them more agile in the air so they are more successful hunters, especially when they are chasing smaller prey. Since the eaglets can only eat small prey when they are young, it is best that the male does all the hunting for the family in these early days.

Feeding the Family

The mother eagle stays in the nest with her chicks for most of the time, until they have grown enough feathers to keep warm on their own. Then she joins the male in hunting for food. By this time, there is probably only one eaglet left alive, but it is growing fast and needs a lot of food.

▼ The eaglet will soon have to fend for itself, when its mother stops cutting up its food.

The food that the parents collect for the growing eaglet is the same as they eat themselves. Grouse and mountain hares, fawns, squirrels and even lizards make up the family's diet. When they are feeding a small eaglet, the parent eagles try to bring back birds, because their meat is tender and easy for the young bird to digest. Eagles rarely kill birds in mid-air, although they can sometimes snatch a grouse while it is taking off. Mostly, they take birds by surprise while they are still perched, usually on the ground.

After the eaglet has fed, it sprawls across the nest to sleep with its crop stuffed with food. Its mother now has a chance to feed herself, and perhaps fly around her territory, although she never goes far from the nest. She often comes back carrying a sprig of heather or a leafy twig, which she adds to the nest. When you see an eagle doing this regularly, it is a good sign that she has an eaglet in the nest.

▼ This male golden eagle in Alaska has caught a bird called a white-tailed ptarmigan (pronounced TAH-muh-guhn).

Growing Up

When the eaglet is four weeks old, the first quills of its proper feathers begin to appear. Two or three weeks later, the new feathers cover its down completely, except for a few tufts on its head. The eaglet is now about half-grown, and it begins to get ready to leave the nest.

First, the eaglet has to learn to feed itself. When its father brings food, its mother no longer tears it up but leaves the eaglet to manage for itself. To do this, the young bird has to learn to hold the meat with its foot while it tears the food with its beak. Soon, the eaglet can eat anything its parents bring.

▲ The eaglet needs plenty of food so it can grow a full set of feathers before leaving the nest. This eaglet is nearly eleven weeks old.

When the eaglet is eight weeks old, its life begins to change. Its father no longer brings food as regularly as he used to. On some days he brings none at all, and on others he might bring two or three dead animals and drop them in the nest. The eaglet can help itself whenever it is hungry. It spends the rest of the time preening its new feathers and flapping its wings.

When it is nearly three months old, the eaglet is fully fledged, which means it has grown a complete set of feathers. The last to grow are the flight feathers in its wings and tail. The breast muscles that move its wings need a lot of exercise to make them strong enough for the eaglet to fly for the first time. So the young bird starts to spend time teetering on the edge of the nest, flapping its wings.

▼ The eaglet may be going nowhere, but it is developing the powerful breast muscles that it will need for flying.

Learning to fly

Gusts of wind occasionally get under the eaglet's outstretched wings, lifting it a little off the nest. For the first week or so, when this happens, the eaglet folds its wings and drops back into the nest. It has been well-fed by its parents and at this age it is too heavy to fly, often even heavier than its mother. The eaglet's constant flapping exercises help to change some of its fat into flight muscles. One day, it lets the wind lift it above the edge of the nest until it can no longer drop back to safety, and finds itself flying for the first time.

▼ The spread feathers at the end of a soaring eagle's wings act like little extra wings, to give it additional lift.

20

HOW BIRDS FLY

When birds hold out their wings, the air passing above and below them creates an upward pressure, which holds them up in the air as they glide along, even if they hold their wings perfectly still. To drive themselves along they flap their wings, creating a swimming action.

The eaglet's first flight is short and rather clumsy. It glides most of the way, occasionally flapping and often losing its balance, until it lands awkwardly. This is usually on the ground, sometimes several hundred feet (meters) away from the nest. However with each attempt, the eaglet gains more balance and gradually improves its flying skills.

Now that the eaglet has left the nest it will never return. The great pile of twigs and branches the nest was made of will lie empty, perhaps for two or three years, until the parent eagles return to use it once more.

▲ After an awkward first few tries, the young eagle will soon be able to fly.

Leaving home

After the eaglet has left the nest, its parents must feed it for another two or three months. By the age of four months the young eagle is fully grown, but it still can't fly well enough to catch food for itself. So the eagle sits on the ground or in trees in its parents' territory, waiting for them to bring it food. They help it train for later life by bringing it live prey, which the eaglet has to kill for itself.

By crushing these small animals in its increasingly powerful claws, the eaglet begins to get the feel of killing. At the same time, it takes part in playful mid-air tussles with its parents.

▼ If the young eagle cannot find food when its parents drive it off, it will die.

The adults pretend to attack the young eaglet as it flies, swooping down on it or sometimes even rolling upside-down beneath it and grabbing its claws in their own. The eaglet joins in enthusiastically, soaring and diving, rolling and swooping with its parents in the sky. These spectacular aerobatics are good practice for the flying skills that will soon let the young hunter catch its own prey.

By now it is late autumn, usually October, and the golden eagles' breeding cycle is coming to an end. The parent birds will soon be preparing for the next season, getting ready to produce another clutch of eggs. The young eagle would be in the way, so at the age of about six months, its parents drive it off to fend for itself. This is a crucial period in the young bird's life and many golden eagles starve to death before they make their first successful kill.

▲ The eagle eyes of the parent birds will find their young even if they are some way from the nest.

The First Hunt

When it begins to hunt, the young eagle has to recognize what is food and what is not. It helps that its parents brought it live squirrels or grouse while they were feeding it away from the nest. This means the young eagle knows that food is something that struggles and has a life of its own, not just a piece of furry or feathery meat.

The eagle's first meals may be very basic, perhaps tiny mice or even large insects. It needs anything that contains protein and fat, which will keep it alive while it is learning to hunt. Soon, though, the young bird will become skillful enough to catch the golden eagle's usual diet—mice, rats, rabbits, small deer, and other mammals.

▶ A rabbit makes a good meal for a young eagle, and on open ground it is relatively easy to catch.

GOLDEN EAGLE FOOD CHAIN

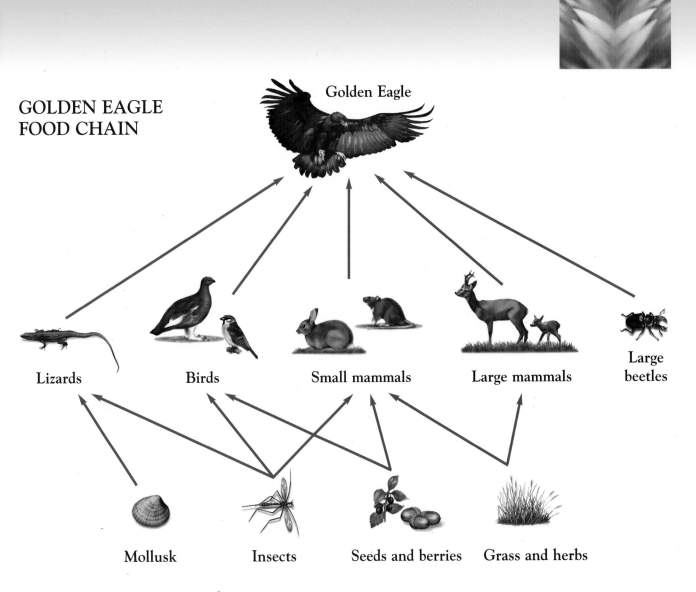

Golden Eagle

Lizards

Birds

Small mammals

Large mammals

Large beetles

Mollusk

Insects

Seeds and berries

Grass and herbs

It can catch and kill the young of larger animals, such as mountain goats in North America and chamois in Europe. It can also kill birds as small as larks and sparrows or as big as grouse, and even sometimes geese and swans.

Sometimes golden eagles take small calves or lambs from farmers' flocks. If food is scarce, they will eat carrion that they find dead on the ground, including calves and lambs that have died from sickness or injury.

▲ The golden eagle's main prey animals are mammals, ranging in size from mice to deer. It catches rabbits and rats everywhere, along with prairie dogs in North America and lemmings in northern Europe.

▲ A golden eagle can see about eighty times better than a chicken.

HEAD MOVEMENT

Birds of prey have such large eyes that they can hardly move them at all in their sockets. To follow a moving target, they must move their heads. Owls have even bigger and less mobile eyes, and because of this they have the most flexible necks of all birds.

Eagle Eyes

Golden eagles, like most other birds of prey, have excellent eyesight. They can see about eight times better than humans, using the most sensitive part of their eye, called the fovea. Most animals, including humans, have only one fovea in each eye, but golden eagles and other birds of prey have two.

Like all birds, since its eyes are on the sides of the eagle's head, each produces a different picture. The eagle's second fovea means that as well as looking sideways with each eye, it can see straight ahead as well, using both eyes at once. This is called binocular vision, and it allows eagles to judge distance very well. Since they dive on their prey, it is very important for eagles to be able to judge distance quickly and accurately. If they made a mistake, they might crash into the ground.

Their excellent eyesight means that golden eagles, like other birds of prey, can watch the ground closely as they glide over their hunting territory. They usually fly quite low, but they can spot small animals moving on the ground and prepare to attack long before their prey can see them.

▶ A bird of prey can see two different views with each eye. Each central fovea receives a wide picture, while the extra fovea enables the bird to see forwards.

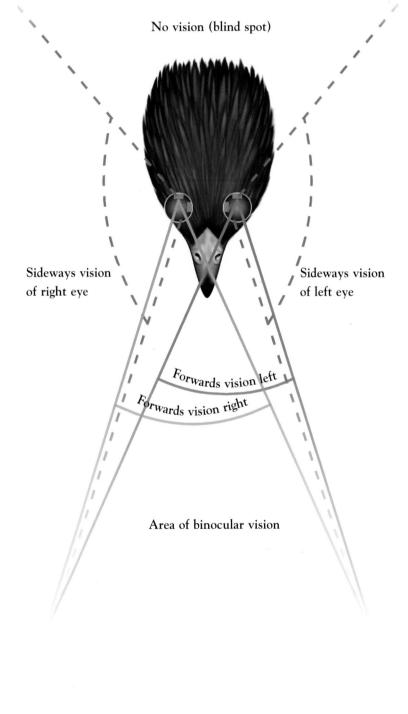

No vision (blind spot)

Sideways vision of right eye

Sideways vision of left eye

Forwards vision left

Forwards vision right

Area of binocular vision

27

Hunting techniques

Golden eagles do not always hunt alone. When they are hunting deer, for example, they often work in pairs. The first eagle dives on the herd, causing them to scatter, while the second follows 328 feet (100 meters) behind, waiting to pick up any young animal that becomes separated from the herd in the panic caused by the first bird's attack. The two eagles then feed on the prey together.

OSPREY FEET

Ospreys are birds of prey that look similar to golden eagles. They have very special feet to help them to catch fish. The soles of their toes are covered with rough scales to get a grip on their slippery prey, and one of their front toes can be turned round and used as a back toe, to improve their grip even more.

Once a golden eagle has seen its prey on the ground, it pounces on it very quickly, striking with its talons outstretched. The eagle has one toe at the back of each foot, and three at the front. As the back toe hits the prey, the three front toes grip tightly, and all four talons spear deep into the victim's body. The shock of the blow is often enough to kill the prey animal, but if it is still alive, the eagle uses its sharp, hooked bill to finish it off.

◀ The powerful hooked talons on its back toes are the golden eagle's main killing weapons.

The next weapon to be used is the eagle's broad wings. They provide enough lift to enable the eagle to carry even quite heavy prey back to its nest, or to a place where it can eat it undisturbed.

The eagle uses the hooked point of its bill to tear off fur or feathers and then strips of skin, to reveal the flesh underneath. It then slices into the meat using the razor-sharp edges of its bill, which work like curved knives.

▼An osprey leaps out of the water after diving in to catch a fish.

Becoming an Adult

The young golden eagle is already fully grown when it leaves the nest. But it will be several years before it becomes an adult. It spends its first winter in the juvenile feathers that it grew while it was in the nest. Unlike the adults, which are almost completely dark brown except for the golden wash on their heads, the young bird has a bright white patch at the base of its tail and white patches along the middle of its wings.

▼ A young golden eagle wears bright white "badges" on its wings and tail. Its dark head shows that this bird is about one year old.

MOULTING

Some birds, such as geese, moult all their flight feathers at once. During the summer, this means that adult geese cannot fly until they have grown new wing and tail feathers. Eagles must be able to fly well all year round to find food, so they moult only a few flight feathers at a time. Their wings and tail always have enough feathers for them to fly properly, but because of this a complete moult takes several months.

The juvenile plumage is like a badge. It shows other eagles that the young bird is not yet an adult, which means it is less of a threat to them than other adults. This may make it possible for the eaglet to hunt in another pair of eagles' territory, without being driven away.

The young eagle begins to moult and change from its first juvenile plumage when it is about one year old, in April. The whole process can take until October before the change is complete. When it is finished, the young bird still bears the white badge on its wings and tail, although it also has a dull golden wash on its head and neck, and its body feathers are less streaky. It must moult three more times before it has the complete adult uniform, when it is four-and-a-half-years old.

Now it is time for the young eagle to find and defend a territory of its own, and to start looking for a mate with which to spend the rest of its life.

Territory and Courtship

As the young eagle looks for its own territory, it will have to find a place that is not already patrolled by an established pair. Eagles do not fight over their territories. By flying high and often over the large area that they control, the owners of a territory warn any other golden eagle that the place is occuppied.

Once it has found a place of its own, the young eagle soars above it until another young eagle of the opposite sex flies nearby. Any bird that is looking for a territory will also be looking for a mate, because once eagles have found a partner, they stay together for life. When the two young strangers meet, they begin to court.

▲ A young eagle may have to search for years before finding an empty territory. The pale marks on its wings may stop adults seeing it as too much of a threat.

The courtship of the golden eagle is spectacular to watch. The male and the female fly together day after day, rolling and diving much as they did with their parents when they were learning to fly. It looks as if each is trying to show the other how good they are at aerobatics. Perhaps they are also showing how good they will be at collecting food for the young, because a good flier will also be a good hunter.

By February of the young eagle's fifth year, it will have established a territory and found a mate. Now it is time to choose the site of their first nest.

▼ A male and female golden eagle in their nest. Male golden eagles are ten percent smaller than females and twenty percent lighter.

Nesting

In rocky country, golden eagles nest on cliff ledges, often in a shallow cave or under an overhang that will keep the rain off. Where there are no cliffs, they nest in tall trees. Nest-building begins in March.

The pair work very hard on their first nest, gathering twigs and even quite large sticks, and piling them on to the chosen nest site. Golden eagles are big and strong enough to tear small branches off trees, laying them on the nest with the green leaves still attached. The pair will use this nest many times during the years to come, adding new material each time, so it will become very big. During their life together, the eagles will build two or three other nests in their territory, so that they never need to use the same nest two years running. This probably guards against nest parasites, which would harm their chicks.

▲ No one really knows why female eagles fetch so many twigs when they have young in the nest.

▶ Eagles like this one, in the Rocky Mountains of Colorado, keep a sharp look-out over their territory. Display flights will drive intruders away.

By the end of March, the nest is ready for the female's eggs. The golden eagles begin a life of bringing up eaglets, into a world that is not always friendly towards them.

EAGLE NEST

After a pair of golden eagles has added twigs and sticks to it year after year, their nest can be as big as 6 feet (1.8 meters) in diameter and 5 feet (1.5 meters) deep. The biggest eagle nest ever seen was used by a pair of bald eagles in Florida, for 35 years. It was 9.5 feet (2.9 meters) wide and 19.7 feet (6 meters) deep. A similar-sized bald eagle nest in Ohio weighed nearly 2 tons.

Eagles and People

Thoughout history, the golden eagle has fascinated people with its hunting techniques and aerobatics, and they have held an important place in the mythology of many cultures. Legend tells how the ancient Aztecs honored the golden eagle so much that they built the ancient city of Tenochtitlán on the spot where one landed. Golden eagles have been used as a symbol of strength, courage and power on the totem poles of Native Americans, the flags of the Roman army, and by Russian and Austrian emperors.

▼ The young eagle did not kill this deer, which probably died a natural death in the snow. But it takes the chance of scavenging the remains.

EAGLE MYTHS

There are stories in many countries of eagles carrying off human babies, usually while the mother was busy in the fields, leaving her infant lying on the ground nearby. None of the stories have ever been proved to be true, but they add to the fear of eagles, and therefore to their persecution by people who believe the stories.

◀ A model of the eagle symbol of a Roman legion shows it holding thunderbolts in its claws.

Fear of eagles

Scientists call birds of prey "raptors," from the Latin word *raptare* meaning "to seize," or rob. Eagles have been regarded as thieves for a very long time. In the past, farmers believed that eagles were stealing their lambs and small calves. This may have been true occasionally, but golden eagles usually keep away from people and farms. They prefer to hunt undisturbed. However, if there are sick or dead animals lying in a field, the eagles sometimes scavenge the corpses. Farmers seeing this might have thought the eagles had killed the animals in the first place.

Threats

In the wild, golden eagles can live up to twenty-five years. Being at the top of their food chain, they have no natural enemies. Their greatest enemies are people, who threaten the golden eagle with illegal hunting, destruction of its habitat and poisoning by pesticides. In the past, eagles were killed to protect farm animals and game birds such as grouse. The killing still goes on, although it is now illegal in almost all countries.

Some eagles are killed by traps. Others are killed by poison, often by accident. If eagles eat poisoned bait put down to kill foxes or wolves, it can kill them. Sometimes they might catch and eat an animal that has eaten poison. When this happens, the eagle will die.

▼ Poison kills many eagles, often by accident when the deadly bait is set for wolves or foxes.

▲ These are the eggs of birds of prey, collected in the nineteenth century. Such collections are now illegal in private hands. This one is in a museum.

Sport and hobbies

In some southern European countries, such as Italy, shooting eagles is a traditional sport in spring and autumn, when many eagles migrate to or from their breeding grounds. The sport is banned by law but it is very hard to stop.

Another serious cause of harm to golden eagles, and to all other rare birds, is egg-collecting. It was once considered a respectable hobby, but when people realized how it affected eagles in the wild, it was banned. However, there are still people who are prepared to pay a lot of money for rare eggs, so there are people who will go out to collect them.

Habitat Loss and Pesticides

Over the last 200 years, farming has spread to highland areas and forests have been cut down for timber. This has destroyed much of the golden eagle's territory and their numbers have fallen.

Even worse, in the 1950s, farmers started using chemicals called pesticides on their crops. Pesticides kill pests such as slugs and insects, which damaged crops. Two pesticides, called DDT and dieldrin, were thought to be a great success. However, no one realized what harm they were doing to birds, especially birds of prey.

▼ This plane is spraying pesticides over farmland.

PESTICIDE POISON

In the 1970s, scientists discovered that eagles that had collected the pesticides DDT and dieldrin in their bodies lay eggs with very thin shells. The eggs broke before they could hatch, which meant that a pair of eagles poisoned by these pesticides could not produce young. DDT also harms eagles' central nervous system.

▲ A dead embryo from a golden eagle egg. It probably died because its mother had absorbed too much pesticide from her food.

Pesticides stay in the bodies of the animals that eat them. This means that pesticides used to kill insects are passed on to the animals who eat the insects. When other animals eat the insect-eaters, they too collect the poison, so it passes up the food chain. Eagles are at the top of the food chain, so they can collect a large dose during a year's feeding. The amount of poison might not be enough to kill the eagles, but it makes it very difficult for them to breed.

Protecting the golden eagle

Protecting against loss of habitat, pesticide poisoning and illegal hunting is not easy. Habitat can be protected by setting up wildlife reserves, where human activities are kept to a minimum. There are many wildlife reserves throughout the golden eagle's range, where it can nest and hunt without being disturbed by people.

Pesticide poisoning has become less serious now that people have realized the harm that they did to eagles in the 1950s and 1960s. Harmful pesticides are now banned in most developed countries, although they are still used in some poorer countries. New pesticides are tested carefully before they are released, to make sure that they do not harm wildlife, including eagles.

▼ If farmers only knew, eagles are their friends, killing thousands of animals that are pests of their crops or livestock. This eagle has killed a fox.

Illegal killing of eagles is more difficult to control. Passing laws against killing eagles does not work if people believe they are in the right. Farmers can be encouraged not to kill eagles if they learn that golden eagles kill more pests such as rabbits, rats and mice than young farm animals. They can protect their young animals by keeping them under cover until they are too big for the eagles to catch.

▲ Fixing wing tags to young golden eagles before they fly helps to follow their development. The tags will fall out next time the eagle moults.

The main way of protecting golden eagles might be to make sure that everyone learns about them, so they can admire them as they soar in the skies.

Golden Eagle Life Cycle

1 > A female eagle lays up to three eggs, called a clutch, in her nest. The parents take turns incubating the eggs.

2 > About 40–45 days after they were laid, the eggs begin to hatch. The chicks break through the eggshell using their egg-tooth. Even if all the eggs hatch, only one eaglet survives to be fed by its parents.

3 > When it first leaves the nest, the young eagle cannot fly well enough to hunt, so its parents bring it live prey for it to kill.

4 When it is about six months old, its parents drive off the young eagle and it has to hunt for its own food.

5 When it is about five years old, the young eagle begins to look for a territory of its own, and a mate with which to spend the rest of its life.

6 When it finds a mate, the pair of eagles work together building their first nest, and raising their own eaglets.

Glossary

Aerobatics (air-uh-BAT-iks) The performance of movements in the air.

Brood (brood) Keep chicks warm on the nest.

Carrion (KAHR-ee-uhn) Dead and decaying flesh.

Clutch (Kluhch) A nest of eggs.

Courtship (KORT-ship) Behavior that helps an animal to win a mate.

Crop (Krop) The part of a bird's gut between its mouth and its stomach, where food is stored and prepared for digestion.

Down Soft, fluffy feathers that trap air and keep a bird warm.

Food chain (food chayn) A sequence in which plants are eaten by small animals, which are eaten by larger animals, which are eaten in turn by even larger animals.

Fovea (FO-vee-uh) A small spot in the center of the eye, where vision is sharpest.

Habitat (HAB-uh-tat) The natural home for an animal or plant.

Incubate (ING-kyuh-bate) To keep eggs warm so that they will hatch.

Migrate (MYE-grate) To move from one area to another as the seasons change.

Moult (mohlt) Lose old feathers and grow new ones.

Parasites (PA-ruh-site) Small animals that live on other animals, often sucking their blood.

Pesticides (PESS-tuh-side) Substances that kill pests such as slugs and insects, which damage crops.

Plumage (PLOO-mij) A bird's feathers.

Preening Combing and grooming feathers to keep them in good condition.

Prey (pray) An animal that is killed and eaten by other animals.

Territory (TER-uh-tor-ee) The area that is defended and controlled by an animal.

Further Information

Organizations to Contact

American Eagle Foundation
P.O. Box 2498
Vancouver, Washington 98668
Tel: (360) 256-0436
Website: www.eagles.org

National Wildlife Federation
8925 Leesburg Pike
Vienna, VA 22184
Tel: (703) 790-4000
Website: www.nwf.org

Websites

PBS Kids
www.pbs.org
Find out about golden eagles
and other birds of prey.

The Discovery Channel
www.discovery.com
Use the search engine to
find information about
golden eagles.

Books to Read

The Animal Kingdom: A guide to Vertebrate Classification and Biodiversity by Kathryn Whyman (Raintree/Steck-Vaughn, 1999)

What's the Difference: Birds by Stephen Savage (Raintree/Steck-Vaughn, 2000)

What is a Bird? by Robert Snedden (Little Brown & Co, 1997)

Index

Page numbers in **bold** refer to photographs or illustrations.

14